WILD WICKED WONDERFUL

TOP 10: MOMS

By Virginia Loh-Hagan

⊖ 45th Parallel Press

Published in the United States of America by Cherry Lake Publishing
Ann Arbor, Michigan
www.cherrylakepublishing.com

Content Adviser: Stephen Ditchkoff, Professor of Wildlife Ecology and Management, Auburn University, Alabama
Reading Adviser: Marla Conn MS, Ed., Literacy specialist, Read-Ability, Inc.
Book Designer: Melinda Millward

Photo Credits: ©EMPPhotography/iStockphoto, cover, 1, 19; ©Jane Rix/Shutterstock.com, 5; ©PHOTOCREO Michal Bednarek/Shutterstock.com, 6; ©Xiebiyun/Shutterstock.com, 6; ©Four Oaks/Shutterstock.com, 6; ©Artush/Shutterstock.com, 7; ©TakinPix/Thinkstock, 8; ©dangdumrong/Shutterstock.com, 8; ©Klaus Hollitzer/Thinkstock, 8; ©orldswildlifewonders/Shutterstock.com, 9; ©Leenvdb/Shutterstock.com, 10; ©Saddako/iStockphoto, 10; ©Rudy Umans/Shutterstock.com, 11; ©Chris Johns/National Geographic Creative, 12; ©GUDKOV ANDREY/Shutterstock.com, 14; ©FloridaStock/Shutterstock.com, 14; ©Shvaygert Ekaterina/Shutterstock.com, 14; ©outdoorsman/Shutterstock.com, 15; ©Outdoorsman/Dreamstime.com, 16; ©Maggy Meyer/Shutterstock.com, 18; ©Alexey Osokin/Shutterstock.com, 18; ©drferry/Thinkstock, 18; ©Goddard_Photography/iStockphoto, 20; ©KiltedArab/Thinkstock, 20; ©Kjersti Joergensen/Shutterstock.com, 20; ©moodboard/Thinkstock, 21; ©Artushfoto/Dreamstime.com, 22; ©Ekaterina Pokrovsky/Shutterstock.com, 22; ©Tui De Roy/ Minden Pictures/Newscom, 23; ©fieldwork/Shutterstock.com, 24; ©David Osborn/Shutterstock.com, 24, 25; ©elnavegante/Shutterstock.com, 24; ©aaltair/Shutterstock.com, 26; ©Adam Ke/Shutterstock.com, 26; ©TheSP4N1SH/iStockphoto, 26; ©Stubblefield Photography/Shutterstock.com, 27; ©Jeff Rotman/Getty Images, 28; ©AppStock/Shutterstock.com, 29; ©Neil Bradfield/ Getty Images, 30; ©Robin Lund/Alamy Stock Photo, 31

Graphic Element Credits: ©tukkki/Shutterstock.com, back cover, front cover, multiple interior pages; ©paprika/Shutterstock.com, back cover, front cover, multiple interior pages; ©Silhouette Lover/Shutterstock Images, multiple interior pages

45th Parallel Press is an imprint of Cherry Lake Publishing.

Library of Congress Cataloging-in-Publication Data

Names: Loh-Hagan, Virginia, author.
Title: Top 10—moms / by Virginia Loh-Hagan.
Other titles: Moms
Description: Ann Arbor : Cherry Lake Publishing, 2016. | Series: Wild wicked wonderful |
    Includes bibliographical references and index.
Identifiers: LCCN 2015050721| ISBN 9781634710978 (hardcover) | ISBN 9781634711968 (pdf) |
    ISBN 9781634712958 (pbk.) | ISBN 9781634713948 (ebook)
Subjects: LCSH: Parental behavior in animals—Juvenile literature.
Classification: LCC QL762 .L643 2016 | DDC 591.56/3—dc23
LC record available at https://lccn.loc.gov/2015050721

Printed in the United States of America
Corporate Graphics

About the Author

Dr. Virginia Loh-Hagan is an author, university professor, former classroom teacher, and curriculum designer. She dedicates this book to Phyllis Dunn, the best and fiercest mom in the world. She lives in San Diego with her very tall husband and very naughty dogs. To learn more about her, visit www.virginialoh.com.

TABLE OF CONTENTS

Introduction 4

Chapter one
Elephants 6

Chapter two
Koala Bears 8

Chapter three
Alligators 10

Chapter four
Polar Bears 14

Chapter five
Cheetahs 16

Chapter six
Orangutans 20

Chapter seven
Red-Knobbed Hornbills 22

Chapter eight
Elephant Seals 24

Chapter nine
Octopuses 26

Chapter ten
Sea Lice 30

Consider This!.. 32
Glossary.. 32
Index.. 32

INTRODUCTION

Animals have babies. Babies ensure **survival** of the **species**. Survive means to live. Species means groups of animals. More babies mean more animals.

Baby animals are cute. But they're helpless. They're little. They don't have any skills. They're **prey**. Prey are hunted as food. Babies need help. They need dads. They need moms.

Animal moms are special. Some protect. Some care. Some teach. But some don't. Some leave their babies. Some are dangerous.

Some animal moms are extreme. Some of the most exciting moms are in the animal world!

Maternal instincts refers to the things moms feel and do without even thinking about it.

chapter one
ELEPHANTS

Elephants live in Africa and Asia. They live together in **herds**. Herds are family groups. Herds are made up of grandmothers, moms, and daughters. There aren't any adult males. The **matriarch** is in charge. Matriarch means the oldest female. She's in charge until she dies.

Moms are **pregnant** for 21 months. This is a long time! Pregnant means having babies grow inside bodies. Moms give birth to 220-pound (100 kilograms) babies. Elephant babies are the biggest babies on land.

Baby elephants are called calves.

Herds take care of each other's babies. Baby elephants get a lot of attention. They can't see well. They only drink milk. They need their moms. Moms work together. They protect babies.

chapter two
KOALA BEARS

Koala bears live in Australia. They live in trees. They eat poisonous leaves. They have special eating systems. Their stomachs have **bacteria**. Bacteria are like bugs living in bodies. They fight the poison.

But koala babies don't have these bacteria. Moms help babies. Moms eat a lot. They make a special poop. It's called **pap**. It has a lot of bacteria. Babies eat this pap. The pap is runny and wet. It can get messy.

Babies eat it for a month. This is how they get bacteria. After eating pap, babies switch to eating leaves.

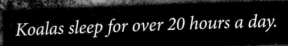

Koalas sleep for over 20 hours a day.

Chapter three

ALLIGATORS

Alligators live in the United States and China. They **mate** in June. Mate means make babies. They make nests in July. They use mud. They use plants. They use sticks. Moms lay 10 to 50 eggs. They cover the eggs. Over time, their nests rot. This creates heat. The heat keeps eggs warm. So, they don't have to sit on the eggs. They stay outside the nests. They protect. They do this for 2 months.

Moms listen for sounds from the eggs. They'll hear grunts in September. They dig out the eggs. They help break the shells. They put the eggs in their mouths. They press down. This cracks the eggs.

Alligator moms usually mate with one dad each breeding season.

Alligators have about 80 sharp teeth.

Moms help their **hatchlings**. Hatchlings are baby alligators. Moms have powerful jaws. They have many sharp teeth. They gently lift their babies. They carry them to the water. They carry them in their mouths!

The mouth of an alligator mom is the safest place for babies. Babies also rest on their mom's heads. They rest on their moms' backs. Babies stay close to their moms. They form **pods**. Pods are family groups. Moms protect their babies for about a year.

Sometimes, babies are in danger. They cry. They get their moms' attention. Moms come. They keep danger away.

DID YOU KNOW...?

- Mother's Day is a holiday. It celebrates mothers. It was founded by Anna Jarvis.

- Animal moms care for their babies. Some have to stop caring after a while. They stop when they get pregnant again. Their attention switches to the new babies. That's tough love!

- The temperature of alligator eggs determines gender. If the temperature is less than 86 degrees Fahrenheit (30 degrees Celsius), the eggs become females. If the temperature is above 93°F (34°C), the eggs become males.

- Female orangutans visit their moms until they're age 16.

- Elephant seals' milk has 15 times more fat than human milk. It has 25 times more fat than cow's milk.

chapter four
POLAR BEARS

Polar bears are loners. They live in the Arctic. It's hard to find a mate. So, it's hard for moms to get pregnant.

Polar bears mate around hunting grounds. Dads follow moms. They can track them for 60 miles (96.5 kilometers). They fight for the moms. Dads and moms stay together for a week.

Pregnant moms are on their own. They find food. They need to gain 400 pounds (181.4 kg) of fat. They double their weight. They store food in their bodies. They need

Polar bear moms usually have two babies.

enough for themselves and their growing babies. If they don't gain weight, their bodies will **absorb** the babies. Absorb means to take in.

Polar bear babies won't leave their moms for at least 2 years.

Moms make a den. They dig tunnels. They dig out rooms. They fall into a deep sleep. They give birth while in the den.

Moms are about 1,000 pounds (453.5 kg). Their babies are 1 pound (0.5 kg). Babies are blind. They don't have teeth. They're covered with soft hair. Babies cling to their moms' fur. They do this to stay warm. They do this for protection.

Moms **nurse** their babies. Nurse means to give milk. Moms' fat turns into milk. The milk is very rich. Babies drink this milk.

Moms and babies leave the den. Moms need to eat. They take a long walk together. Moms teach babies how to hunt.

HUMANS DO WHAT?!?

Some traditional Chinese women practice *zuo yuezi*. This means "sitting the month." After giving birth, these Chinese women confine themselves. They lock themselves up. They do this for about a month. This practice is meant to help new mothers recover. It's meant to restore balance to their bodies. There are many rules. They can't go outside. They can't shower. They can't drink cold drinks. They can't eat raw fruits or vegetables. They have to keep warm. They have to stay in bed. They can eat hot soups. For example, they can eat a soup made with pig's feet and peanuts. They can eat a fish oil soup. These soups help their bodies make milk.

chapter five

CHEETAHS

Cheetahs live in Africa. They're the fastest land animals in the world.

Moms find a **lair**. Lairs are resting places. Moms give birth in lairs. Moms have about three or four **cubs**. Cubs are babies.

Moms hunt every day. They have hungry cubs to feed. They can't leave their cubs. So, they teach their cubs to hunt. At 6 weeks old, cubs watch and learn.

Moms track prey. They chase down prey. They kill prey.

Cheetah moms don't get any help from dads.

They feed their cubs.

Moms teach their cubs survival skills. They leave as soon as cubs can hunt. Moms start new families.

Chapter six

ORANGUTANS

Orangutans are part of the great apes family. They live on Southeast Asian islands. They're the largest animals to live in trees.

Moms build nests in trees. They build new nests every night. They build over 30,000 homes in a lifetime. Their nests are strong. They're safe. They're used for sleeping. They protect their babies.

Moms gather tree leaves. They bend branches. They make a strong base. They tuck in small twigs. They make beds. The beds are 15 to 100 feet (4.6 to 30.5 meters) above ground.

Orangutans are four times stronger than humans.

Babies cling tightly to their moms. Babies don't want to fall.

Moms have strong bonds with their babies. Babies need moms for food and travel. Moms teach babies how to survive.

Chapter seven
RED-KNOBBED HORNBILLS

Red-knobbed hornbills live in Sulawesi. It's an island in Southeast Asia.

They're extreme stay-at-home moms. They make nests inside trees. They use their own poop. They use feathers. They use food. They seal themselves inside. The nests are like smelly concrete prisons. Moms make a tiny hole. That's how they pee and poop.

Dads roam free. They hunt for food. They **regurgitate** food. They spit the food up. They pass it through the hole.

Red-knobbed hornbills depend on each other. Moms and dads stay together for a while.

Moms stay there for several months. Moms focus on laying eggs. They focus on raising **chicks**. Chicks are baby birds. They protect their chicks. When the chicks are ready they break out of the nest. They fly away.

chapter eight
ELEPHANT SEALS

Elephant seals live by water. They live in California. They live in Antarctica.

Moms live in **harems**. Harems are groups of females. They share one male. One male has about 40 to 50 females in his harem. Dads are four times bigger than moms.

Moms are pregnant 11 months of each year. They eat for two. They store **blubber**. Blubber is fat. Moms have one baby at a time. After they give birth, their fat changes into milk for the baby. They lose 20 pounds (9 kg) every time they nurse. They lose about 600 pounds (272 kg) total.

Elephant seal moms weigh 1,700 pounds (771 kg).

While they nurse, moms don't eat. They live off their blubber.

Moms protect their **pups**. Pups are baby seals. Moms bark.
They use their flippers.

chapter nine

OCTOPUSES

Octopuses live at the bottom of the sea. They have two eyes. They have four pairs of **tentacles**. Tentacles are arms. They have **suctions**. Suctions suck onto things. Octopuses don't have bones. They can squeeze through tight places. Moms use their skills. They do anything to protect their babies.

Moms find a lair. They can lay over 200,000 eggs. They wash their eggs. They use their tentacles. They cover their eggs. They protect their eggs. This takes up all their time. This takes up all their energy. They do this for 40 days.

Octopuses camouflage. They hide.
They change shape, color, and texture.

Octopus moms starve to protect their eggs.

Moms never leave. They're tired. They don't eat. So, they're starving. Some moms eat their own tentacles. Some die from hunger.

Cod are fish. They like eating octopus eggs and babies. Octopus moms become too tired to fight. They let cod eat them instead. They give up their own lives for their babies.

Octopuses don't live that long. Most live for about a year. Dads live for a few months after mating. Moms die shortly after their eggs hatch. They lose their color. Their eyes become cloudy. They get smaller. They get weak. They become easy prey. They don't get to raise their babies.

WHEN ANIMALS ATTACK!

Maureen Lee went on a hike. She took her daughter, Maya. Maya was 3 years old. They were walking their dog. They were picking berries. A cougar pounced on Maya. The cougar was 88 pounds (40 kg). The cougar rolled Maya a couple of times. It had Maya on her back. Its paws were on Maya's head. Lee protected Maya. She put herself between Maya and the cougar. She pushed the cougar away. She picked up Maya. She ran to a nearby house. She said, "I just knew I had to react quick. So, I just jumped in there." Maya had some cuts on her head and arm. But she was okay. Maya asked, "Why didn't the kitty play nice?"

chapter ten
SEA LICE

Sea lice live in warm waters. They live around the Caribbean.
They're marine **parasites**. Parasites live on a host. Sea lice
live on fish. They eat snot, blood, and skin.

Males lure females into their lair. Females can't escape.
They're trapped inside. There can be up to 25 females there.
Males mate with them. The females become pregnant. They
become moms. They have hundreds of babies.

Baby sea lice kill their moms. They chew through their
moms. They chew from inside their bodies out. Moms die.

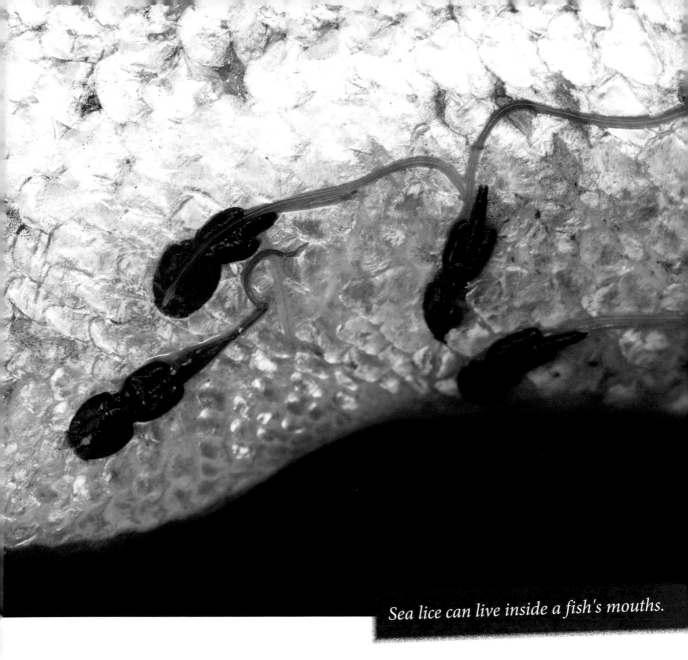

Sea lice can live inside a fish's mouths.

Their bodies split apart. The babies are on their own. Sea lice moms make the extreme **sacrifice**. They give up their lives.

CONSIDER THIS!

TAKE A POSITION! Zoos get very excited about animal babies. Some people don't think wild animals should be kept in zoos. But zoos help keep species alive. Do you think zoos should help animals give birth and raise animals in captivity? Argue your point with reasons and evidence.

SAY WHAT? Read *Extreme Dads*. This is another 45th Parallel Press book by Virginia Loh-Hagan. Compare the dads to the moms in this book. Explain how they are similar. Explain how they are different.

THINK ABOUT IT! Humans share behaviors with animals. In what ways do human moms behave like animal moms?

LEARN MORE!

- Bellows, Melina Gerosa. *Mother's Love: Inspiring True Stories from the Animal Kingdom*. Washington, DC: National Geographic, 2012.
- Berger, Melvin, and Gilda Berger. *101 Animal Babies*. New York: Scholastic, 2013.

GLOSSARY

absorb (ab-ZORB) to take in

bacteria (bak-TEER-ee-uh) tiny organisms living in bodies

blubber (BLUHB-ur) fat

chicks (CHIKS) baby birds

cubs (KUHBZ) baby cheetahs or bears

harems (HAIR-umz) groups of females who share a male

hatchlings (HACH-lingz) babies that come out of eggs

herds (HURDZ) groups of elephants

lair (LAIR) a resting place, like a den

mate (MAYT) to make babies

matriarch (MAY-tree-ark) the oldest female in charge

nurse (NURS) to feed milk to babies

pap (PAP) special poop made by koalas that has a lot of bacteria

parasites (PAR-uh-sites) tiny living things that live on or in animals and feed off them

pods (PAHDZ) family groups

pregnant (PREG-nuhnt) having young growing inside the body

prey (PRAY) animals that are hunted for food

pups (PUHPS) baby seals

regurgitate (re-GURJ-uh-tayt) to spit up food that has been swallowed

sacrifice (SAK-ruh-fice) an offering

species (SPEE-sheez) groups of animals

suctions (SUK-shuhnz) sucking tools

survival (sur-VYE-vuhl) the act of staying alive

tentacles (TEN-tuh-kuhlz) flexible arms that often have suction discs

INDEX

alligators, 10–12, 13
attacks, 29

blubber, 24–25

cheetahs, 13, 18–19

dens, 16

eggs, 10, 13, 23, 26, 28
elephant seals, 13, 24–25
elephants, 6–7

harems, 24
herds, 6, 7

koala bears, 8–9

lair, 18, 26, 30

mating, 10, 11, 14

nests, 20, 22

octopuses, 26–28

orangutans, 13, 20–21

parasites, 30
pods, 12
polar bears, 14–16
predators/prey, 4, 18, 28
pregnancy, 6, 14

red-knobbed hornbills, 22–23

sea lice, 30–31